HUDDERSFIELD PAMPHLETS IN HISTORY AND POLITICS

HP 4

Elizabeth I: Myth and Reality

Keith Dockray

THE POLYTECHNIC OF HUDDERSFIELD

1990

First published 1990

Huddersfield pamphlets in History and Politics are designed to stimulate discussion and to provide an up-to-date view of scholarly debate in their field. They are intended for use by A-level students but will also introduce readers at other levels to the topics chosen. Suggestions for additional titles are welcomed, and should be sent to the general editors.

Printed and published by the Department of Humanities, The Polytechnic of Huddersfield, Queensgate, HUDDERSFIELD HD1 3DH

General Editors: J.A.G. Roberts, K. Laybourn & P.L. Woodfine

Telephone enquiries: (0484) 422288 ext. 2359

ISBN
0905434269

ELIZABETH I : MYTH AND REALITY

Keith Dockray

Elizabeth I is not only one of the most fascinating and written about of English monarchs but also among the most widely admired - as a woman who, against all the odds, firmly set her personal imprint on the times in which she lived and directed her country's fortunes (at a very difficult period in its history) in a notably wise and prudent fashion. Fortunately, she was granted a long reign in which to carve out this enviable reputation (amounting to almost 45 years in all, 1558-1603), and the so-called Elizabethan age is often portrayed as no less meaningful than that taking its name from Elizabeth's even longer-lived nineteenth-century successor Queen Victoria. Since the early 1950s, moreover, enthusiasm for – and interest in – all things Elizabethan has been significantly stimulated by the fact that we have been living under the nominal rule of a modern-day Elizabeth: indeed, in the first decade or so of Elizabeth II's reign there was a good deal of clap-trap flying around about our present Queen as the inaugurator of a new Elizabethan age – the implication clearly being that the first Elizabethan epoch was a particularly splendid era only too worthy of re-creation.

At the time of her birth there was little reason to think the twentieth-century Elizabeth would ever achieve the English throne – and, oddly enough, the same is true of her sixteenth-century namesake. Henry VIII's unwelcome daughter by Anne Boleyn, she was very soon declared illegitimate and, particularly following her father's death in 1547, her prospects hardly seemed promising: nevertheless, following the deaths in rapid succession of her half-brother Edward VI in 1553 and her half-sister Mary in 1558, Elizabeth I did indeed ascend the English throne – and it did not take long for her reputation as a great Queen to begin to develop, thanks not least to Elizabeth's own very considerable efforts to present herself as a symbol of all that was good and admirable in the eyes of later Tudor men and women. It is abundantly clear, indeed, that Elizabeth and her advisers deliberately set out to encourage the idolisation of her person, most notably through the media of literature and art, and that this was done for a combination of political and propaganda purposes.

The Making of the Myth

The Queen certainly enjoyed flattery and welcomed it, and it was the mark of a successful Elizabethan courtier that he could please her by his attentions; but she was also very aware of the political advantages that might accrue from successful image-projection, believing, in fact, that it was essential for the well-being of her regime that she be regarded as the visible and effective embodiment of the State. In this context, it is clearly necessary to stress the importance of Elizabeth's own personality and ability, particularly in enabling her to count on the loyalty and support of the English people for most of the reign. The Queen herself acknowledged this on several occasions, most notably in her address to the army at Tilbury during the crisis occasioned by the sailing of the Spanish Armada in 1588, and the speech is certainly a splendid illustration of Elizabeth's capacity to project herself. "Let tyrants fear", she declared dramatically, since:

> ... I have always so behaved myself that, under God, I have placed my chiefest strength and safeguard in the loyal hearts and goodwill of my subjects, and therefore, I am come amongst you, to lay down for my God, and for my kingdom, and for my people, my honour and my blood, even in the dust.

"I know", she continued in one of the purple passages of history, that:

> ... I have the body but of a weak and feeble woman; but I have the heart and stomach of a King, and of a King of England too; and think foul scorn that Parma or Spain, or any prince of Europe, should dare to invade the borders of my realm; to which, rather than any dishonour shall grow by me, I myself will be your general, judge and rewarder of every one of your virtues in the field.

No less striking is Elizabeth's speech to Parliament in 1601, two years before she died. "I do assure you", she then declaimed, that:

> ... there is no prince that loves his subjects better, or whose love can counterveil our love ... And though God has raised me high, yet this I count the glory of my crown - that I have reigned with your love.

Elizabeth I was certainly adept at exploiting the mystique of monarchy, thereby both making it more difficult for critics to thwart her wishes and easier for the Queen to shine at Court even after she had grown old and ugly. Elizabeth, in fact, dominated the Court right up to her death, and the splendour of that Court undoubtedly did much to foster the myth of Gloriana in the Queen's lifetime and help make her reign so memorable afterwards. The elaborate and magnificent ritual of the Court made a great impression on contemporaries and was meant to do so. Wherever the Queen happened to be, moreover, such pageantry and ceremonial was maintained, most notably when she set out on progresses. During the summer months Elizabeth frequently undertook tours through the southern shires of her realm when she was able to show herself to a wider public: she made at least 25 during her 45 year reign. The Court accompanied her on these progresses, Elizabeth and her retinue generally staying two or three nights at each of the places where she stopped (happily accepting the hospitality of local nobility and gentry, often at considerable cost to them while usefully minimising expenditure by the Queen herself). Elizabeth clearly did wish to show herself to as many of her subjects as was practically possible, often making impromptu speeches, and demonstrating good humour towards even the lewdest of onlookers: in 1568, indeed, the Spanish ambassador remarked how frequently the Queen ordered her carriage to be taken where the crowds were thickest. And these progresses were nothing if not spectacular and brilliant occasions, Elizabeth considering them an excellent means of promoting loyalty and patriotism. They were usually marked, too, by lavish entertainments: when the Queen visited Robert Dudley Earl of Leicester at Kenilworth in 1575, for instance, intervals between banqueting, dancing and hunting were spent watching firework displays, a water pageant, a masque and several plays (not to mention more mundane frivolities like the sadly ever-popular bear-baiting). Progresses did not take place every year: they were virtually suspended, indeed, in the decade preceding the Armada (although Elizabeth resumed them again in the 1590s). Also, it should be emphasised, progresses were confined to the South and Midlands where the solid bulk of support for the Tudor regime lay: Elizabeth never visited the West Country, Wales or the North and it is no coincidence that the one major rebellion against her, in 1569, was centred in the North (while the southern nobility and gentry remained conspicuously loyal).

Court pageantry and progresses apart, literature and art comprised the other major means whereby Elizabeth was idolised and the cult of Gloriana promulgated. Poets and dramatists were certainly inclined to employ extravagantly fanciful imagery to express the Queen's qualities and sing her praises generally. For William Shakespeare, she was "a pattern to all princes living (and) all that shall succeed"; Ben Jonson hailed her as "Queen and huntress, chaste and fair"; while the playwright Thomas Dekker, writing in 1600, penned an even more fulsome adulation of the Queen as if she were a goddess and her Court a temple where she could be adored:

> Some call her Pandora, some Gloriana, some Cynthia, some Astraea - all by several names to express several loves. Yet all those names make but one celestial body, as all loves meet to create but one soul. I am one of her country, and we adore her by the name of Eliza.

Similar imagery was employed by portrait painters. The so-called Ditchley portrait, for instance, painted when the Queen was some sixty years old, shows her as an ageless and majestic figure, standing on a map of England, her magnificent gown and hair decorated with pearls (symbolising her much vaunted virginity), while a storm rages behind her and a sonnet on her right explains that this is all intended to signify her great power. Portraits, miniatures, engravings and woodcuts of the Queen seem to have been in considerable demand: men and women displayed them in their homes and even carried medallions on their persons as demonstrations of loyalty. In 1563, moreover, a royal proclamation was issued banning representations of her which were of inferior quality; while, in 1596, the destruction was ordered of all unflattering portraits of the now sadly ageing Elizabeth. In fact, as the Queen grew older, it was clearly official policy that she be not portrayed realistically as the pock-marked old woman with a red wig and rotting teeth which she had undoubtedly become; rather, the image of an ever-youthful and always imposing figure continued to be promulgated. Myth fully replaced reality in this respect at least.

Clearly, in her last years, Elizabeth did lose grip to come extent, even if not entirely (as her robust response to the futile rebellion of Robert Devereux Earl of Essex in 1601 shows); certainly, there is evidence that by 1603, despite all the propaganda hype, her popularity was seriously on the wane. Many men heaved a sigh of relief when the Queen at last died in that year and eagerly anticipated the prospect of a King (the first mature male to rule England since Henry VIII's death in 1547). Yet it did not take long for Elizabeth's reputation to revive in the early Stuart period: the behaviour of James I and, still more, Charles I saw to that! In 1621 the lawyer Sir Edward Coke emotionally declared in the House of Commons that "she was the flower of Queens just as the rose is the queen of flowers", while James I's own Secretary of State, Sir Robert Naunton, even went so far as to portray her as both a Protestant champion and a friend of Parliament. In 1628 Sir John Eliot was powerfully moved by the contrast between Elizabeth's prestigious achievements and Charles I's ignominious failures. "You know how she advanced herself", he told the Commons; indeed, how she "advanced the nation in glory and state, enjoyed a full security, and made them (England's enemies) our scorn, who are now made our terror". Even Charles I himself promised the Long Parliament in 1641, the year before the outbreak of Civil War, that it was his intention "to reduce all matters of religion and government to what they were in the purest times of Queen Elizabeth's days".

Early Stuart historians, too, tended to be enthusiastic about the Queen and her achievements. William Camden, for instance, writing in the reign of James I, deliberately set out to celebrate "the memory of that princess (Elizabeth) which, amongst Englishmen, ought ever to be grateful and sacred". The age of Elizabeth, he believed, was a time of great innovation and national achievement; the Queen, he declared, was a woman of stature who promoted Protestantism, defended the realm vigorously and won the devotion of her people; indeed, it was Camden who first tentatively advanced the notion of Elizabeth pursuing a *via media* in politics (an interpretation that was to be taken up again in Victorian times by J.A.Froude and J.R.Green and, in the twentieth century, by J.E. Neale). Edward Hyde, Earl of Clarendon, the Royalist historian of the English Revolution, looked back nostalgically to the prosperity of Elizabeth's reign which, he thought, "shines with so much splendour before our eyes" (in contrast to his own troubled times).

Later seventeenth and eighteenth-century historians, similarly, often saw fit to praise Elizabeth – not least for her firm stand, as they saw it, against Popery both at home and abroad. Rapin in the early eighteenth century, for instance, recognised Elizabeth's admirable qualities as a ruler: interestingly, however, he also declared that "she had a mind to make it believed that she did some things from an excessive love of her people when, in fact, she was led more by her own interest". David Hume, in his *History of England* published at the beginning of George III's reign, recognised that Elizabeth's "qualities as a sovereign are the object of undisputed applause"; yet he identified, as well, a tyrannical element in her rule, even comparing her authoritarian character and tendencies with those of Peter the Great of Russia. Lord Macauley, doyen of early nineteenth-century Whig historians, believed that, although "forms of despotism" prevailed in Elizabeth's reign, the Queen's authority rested on the support and "willing obedience" of her subjects: hence why, he thought, her memory still remained in his own time "dear to the hearts of a free people". Macauley's contemporary, the Roman Catholic John Lingard, was notably less generous in his assessment: intelligent, even courageous, Elizabeth may have been, but she was also irritable, foul-mouthed, tyrannical (especially in the persecution of Catholics) and habitually prone to procrastination. Lingard even questioned the Queen's much publicised virginity, while concluding that a good deal of the success of this excessively parsimonious, obsessively suspicious and chronically authoritarian figure was down to her ministers rather than the Queen herself. J.A.Froude likewise, in the 1860s, found her vacillating and inconsistent; she had, he believed, a profound contempt for Protestantism; and her successes, such as they were, reflected an able group of ministers (especially William Cecil Lord Burghley). Perhaps the most influential of later Victorian historians, as far as Elizabeth's modern reputation is concerned, was John Richard Green (whose immensely popular *Short History of the English People* was first published in 1874). Although he had doubts about her political wisdom on occasion, convinced himself that "no woman ever lived who was so destitute of the sentiment of religion", and detected in her "a passionless indifference" and a "cold, critical intellect" never swayed either by enthusiasm or panic, Green admired the Queen nonetheless as a pragmatist and an advocate of the *via media* at a time when these were just the qualities needed by a divided nation. Tenacious and single-minded in her pursuit of peace, moderation and good government, a master of the arts of conciliation and compromise, she assuredly played "with a hundred courses, fitfully and discursively, as a musician runs his fingers over the keyboard, until she hit suddenly upon the right one".

During the 1890s no fewer than six biographies of Elizabeth I were published (including, most importantly, Bishop Mandell Creighton's 1896 study in which he suggested that "Elizabeth's imperishable claim to greatness" derives from the Queen's "instinctive sympathy with her people"). Even more strikingly, between 1927 and 1936, a further thirteen biographies were published in England. Of these, by far the most important was that by Sir John Neale. His biography of "this amazing Queen" was published in 1934: almost sixty years later it is still in print and must continue to figure in any top ten selection of historical works combining scholarship and readability. Indeed, Elizabeth's modern reputation is essentially J.E.Neale's creation and for many years historians operated very much in its shadow: in 1960, for instance, Joel Hurstfield penned a political biography suggesting that not only did the Queen restore "unity and strength to a divided nation" but also brought England to "within striking distance of the time of her imperial greatness". During the last couple of decades, however, Elizabeth's reputation has waned considerably (at any rate in scholarly circles). J.E.Neale, it is now increasingly felt, himself fell victim to the Queen's not inconsiderable charms and his portrait of her is over-indulgent to say the least. J.P.Kenyon, for one, has remarked on Neale's "uncritical approach to the great Queen" and his "intensely nationalist" stance; he is not impressed, either, with Neale's tendency to view her as both "the great headmistress" and the "lonely embattled ruler of a tiny island" who heroically united the nation against the alien ideology and military aggression of Philip II of Spain. Neville Williams declared, in 1968, that, if the reign of Elizabeth had ended in 1572, it could only have been judged "an unremarkable failure"; Lacey Baldwin Smith, in 1976, found the documents of the reign "laden with unpleasant evidence" of the Queen's "vanity, sarcasm, deceit, ingratitude, parsimony, pride and evil temper"; and, in 1988, Christopher Haigh concluded:

> Queen Elizabeth did not attempt to solve problems, she simply avoided them ... Her refusal to tackle the succession issue, her sale of Crown lands to finance war, and her denial of place and reward to the Essex generation showed how limited was her concern for the future ... Queen Elizabeth may have been God's servant, but she was certainly not her people's.

The Reality

What, then, are we to make of all this? Elizabeth I certainly faced enormous difficulties when, after a notably chequered career and many experiences she was no doubt anxious to forget, she finally achieved the English throne in 1558. For a start, she inherited a potentially lethal religious cocktail (the result of Henry VIII's Reformation, the spread of Protestantism under Edward VI and the Counter Reformation under Mary I): a solution had to be found to this and, once in place, defended from inevitable criticism from those who were bound to be dissatisfied (whatever that solution might be). No less urgent was the need to extricate herself from the complications resulting from her sister Mary's marriage to Philip II of Spain and England's consequent involvement in Continental war; thereafter, she had to respond, in foreign policy, to the continuing Counter Reformation in Western Europe (increasingly spear-headed by Philip II) and its attendant warfare (notably the French Wars of Religion and the Revolt of the Netherlands). She had to grapple as well with the ever-present problems of government finance in an age of inflation – problems that became dire indeed once England and Spain embarked, in 1585, on a war that was to last almost twenty years. And she had to face up to the fact that her subjects in Parliament were increasingly inclined to express themselves strongly on a whole range of matters (such as the

Queen's own marriage, Mary Queen of Scots, the succession, foreign policy and religion) and expected her to respond positively to their criticisms and suggestions.

Let us take religion first. There has been much debate about the Elizabethan Religious Settlement, the nature of the Anglican Church that grew out of it and the seriousness of the threat posed by its critics (whether Roman Catholic or Puritan). Even the Queen's personal religious predilections and their importance have been disputed. Was she, as William Camden suggested, genuinely concerned to promote Protestantism? Was she rather, as J.A.Froude believed, openly contemptuous of Protestantism? Or was she, perhaps, indifferent (sceptical even) in matters of religion? In all probability, as befitted the daughter of Anne Boleyn, she was firmly Protestant from the start; so, too, were those around her; and the settlement of 1559 clearly reflected this in its Protestant character. Although Elizabeth might well have preferred a less Calvinist body of doctrine, she certainly appreciated the political advantages of an all-embracing national church with a membership based on outward conformity rather than deep commitment. Indeed, throughout her reign, she resisted all serious attempts at modification (even if it meant clamping down on Protestant evangelism and preaching, even if it meant suspending Archbishop Grindal for years on end, even if it meant encouraging Archbishop Whitgift's crusade against the minority of nonconforming Puritans). Puritanism was never a real danger to either the Crown or the Anglican Church (whatever the Queen's misgivings). Roman Catholicism clearly was: the Pope excommunicated Elizabeth and called for her removal in 1570; seminary priests and Jesuits mounted a vigorous missionary drive in England; and, following the outbreak of war with Spain, Catholics did appear to many loyalists as a potentially dangerous fifth column. And, although the Queen herself may well have regretted the necessity (and even resisted aggressive anti-Catholic legislation), a campaign amounting to persecution did get underway in the 1580s.

During the first decade or two of the reign, Elizabeth came under considerable pressure to marry; while, throughout it, the succession to the throne remained a bone of contention between the Queen and her critics. Elizabeth was the last Tudor and there was genuine fear that, if she died unmarried and without a legitimate heir of her body, England might dissolve into civil war (as it had in the fifteenth century): such apprehension was highlighted by the Queen's brush with death during a bout of smallpox in 1562 and intensified by the arrival of Mary Queen of Scots in England in 1568 (since she was the obvious successor, even alternative, to Elizabeth). Not that there was any shortage of suitors, particularly in the early years, ranging from Philip II of Spain to Robert Dudley Earl of Leicester (whom Elizabeth might well have married had politics not taken precedence over personal predilection). Clearly, the Queen's resistance to marriage paid off handsomely in a number of cases: the Earl of Arran, a suitor in 1560, subsequently went insane; Erik XIV of Sweden became a homicidal maniac and had to be deposed in 1568; as for the Duke of Alençon (whom Elizabeth affectionately called her little frog during a seemingly ardent courtship in 1579), it is difficult to see how he could ever have been acceptable either at Court or in the country. As it was, Elizabeth never did marry and perhaps she was right: at least she avoided the diplomatic complications marriage to a foreign prince might have brought and the probable factional consequences of taking a native consort. Of course, this left open the succession question and, during the 20 year sojourn of Mary Queen of Scots in England (until Elizabeth finally, and not before time, signed her death warrant in 1587), it clearly was a serious matter indeed – as the series of Catholic plots aimed at putting Mary on the throne made only too apparent. Fortunately, Elizabeth's longevity enabled her to outlive most potential claimants and, once the field was narrowed virtually to Protestant James VI of Scotland alone, the urgency went out of the matter: yet Elizabeth, whether out of pride, pig-headedness or even political perspicacity, could never bring herself formally to name him as her successor.

There has certainly been considerable disagreement among historians about Elizabeth's foreign policy and the degree of skill exercised by the Queen in her relations with foreign powers: indeed, there has even been discussion as to whether she had anything that can truly be called a foreign policy at all or whether what we really have is a series of opportunistic expedients determined by financial considerations as much as anything else. Most argue, however, that whatever was done almost certainly reflected the Queen's own priorities and objectives. R.B.Wernham, perhaps the most eminent of recent writers on the subject, believes she did have a foreign policy, based on clear ends, even if the routes by which she reached her goals were tortuous to say the least: indeed, she had a considerable personal interest in, and understanding of, foreign affairs, as her avid reading and correction of diplomatic documents shows; moreover, when it came to war, she had a better grasp of military matters than most. Yet Elizabeth seems to have entertained no dynastic or territorial ambitions; both she and Philip II put a great deal of effort, over many years, into avoiding out-and-out military confrontation; and, when war finally came in 1585, her aims remained essentially defensive rather than aggressive. Moreover, apart from the defeat of the Spanish Armada in 1588 (where "Protestant winds" played a bigger role than Sir Francis Drake and his fellow sea-dogs), there was little to show for it all in the end: the naval war was a stalemate; so was the campaign in the Netherlands; and Ireland, as so often, proved beyond an English government's ability fully to master. The real significance of the war, arguably, was to highlight Elizabeth's parsimonious tendencies, expose the inadequacies of Tudor government finance and contribute to the Queen's declining popularity in her later years.

Historians have always been fascinated by the role of Parliament in Elizabeth's reign. Indeed, Crown/Parliament relations have been analysed in considerable detail by Sir John Neale in his 2- volume study of *Elizabeth I and her Parliaments* (published in the 1950s). According to Neale, the Elizabethan House of Commons contained a powerful Puritan lobby, political and constitutional conflicts were very much the order of the day, and Parliament was notably vocal on such matters as the urgent need for the Queen to marry in her first decade or more, the danger posed by Mary Queen of Scots in the 1570s and early 1580s, and the manifold shortcomings of government religious, financial and foreign policies for much of the reign. Elizabeth herself is to be admired, on this interpretation, for her long-suffering tolerance and determination to resist the Puritan hot-heads: in 1566 she warned her critics that "I will never be by violence constrained to do anything" and advised them "never to tempt too far a prince's patience"; in 1571 she instructed the Commons in no uncertain terms "to meddle with no matters of state but such as should be proposed to them"; and she frequently exercised her power to veto legislation not to her liking. Yet Sir Robert Naunton believed, in the early seventeenth century, that the differences between Elizabeth and Parliament were less significant than their mutual loyalty; while revisionist historians, notably G.R.Elton and Michael Graves, have recently taken the whole Neale picture apart. Certainly, there is a great danger both of exaggerating the frequency of conflict between Queen and Parliament and underestimating their fundamental harmony of interests: more often than not an atmosphere of compromise prevailed in their relations; the Puritan lobby was not as powerful as Neale thought; and royal management ensured reasonable rapport for most of the time. When conflict did erupt, as in the debate over monopolies in 1601, it was the exception rather than the rule.

The Queen, the Court and the Council – not Parliament – dominated the political life of Elizabethan England. The Queen, of course, was the fount of patronage and the royal Court a magnet for politically ambitious men: yet, contrary to the most frequently advanced interpretation, Elizabeth's Court was not dominated by factional struggle. Rivalries there certainly were (for instance, between William Cecil Lord Burghley and Robert Dudley Earl of Leicester on occasion), but Elizabeth both controlled and manipulated the "many servants to whom I grant my favour" in her own interest for most of the reign: even in her last years the situation never got entirely out of hand. Perhaps Sir Robert Naunton got it right when he wrote, in the early 1630s, that the "principal note" of the Queen's reign was that "she ruled much by factions and parties, which she herself both made, upheld and weakened, as her own great judgment advised". Nevertheless there is evidence of political deterioration in the 1590s and the Queen was hard-pressed to control the tempestuous Robert Devereux Earl of Essex: the Council did increasingly have the character of a self-perpetuating oligarchy; Burghley was backing his son Robert Cecil's political aspirations for all he was worth; and Essex, strong-willed, greedy for power and oblivious to the conventions of the Court, had a positive genius for disruption. Eventually, Essex completely over-stepped the mark, fomented rebellion in 1601, and earned himself a traitor's death.

Conclusion

Clearly, Elizabeth possessed both ability and determination; she had a real capacity to grapple with difficult issues and appreciate the consequences of her actions; and, if necessary, she was even prepared to give way on occasion and modify her policies. Equally clearly,she was an inveterate procrastinator; ever parsimonious and penny-pinching, she yet never tackled the fundamental problems facing her government in an age of inflation; she did not understand, or did not want to understand, even the legitimate political, religious and social aspirations of many of her subjects; and, during her last years, she had no solution to the mounting pressure of economic depression, war taxation and social distress. Perhaps the French ambassador showed real perception when he remarked, in 1597, that Elizabeth's government was now "little pleasing to the great men and nobles, and, if by chance she should die, it is certain that the English would never again submit to the rule of a woman". Indeed, there may even be some justification for the graphic judgment of a seventeenth-century Fifth Monarchist that the Queen was no more than "a sluttish housewife who swept the house but left the dust behind the door".

Bibliography

So much has been written about Elizabeth I that constructing a very brief bibliography is almost impossible. The following six items provide a good start and plenty of indications of how to build on it constructively.

J.E.Neale *Queen Elizabeth I* (1934)

A classic work by a very distinguished historian, scholarly, readable, full of fascinating information and bubbling with ideas, but now recognised as romantic, nationalist and much too kind to Elizabeth. Yet it gripped me as a sixth-former in 1961 and still does.

J. Hurstfield *Elizabeth I and the Unity of England* (1960)

A readable and stimulating political biography, very much in the Neale mould, portraying Elizabeth as restoring unity to a divided nation.

R.L.Greaves (ed.) *Elizabeth I, Queen of England* (1974)

A useful collection of substantial passages from commentaries on Elizabeth I, ranging from William Camden and Sir Robert Naunton (early seventeenth century), John Lingard and J.A.Froude (nineteenth century) to J.E.Neale and Neville Williams (twentieth century).

C. Haigh (ed.) *The Reign of Elizabeth* (1984)

An interesting range of articles on the Elizabethan age, with a perceptive and stimulating introduction by the editor, and including Simon Adams (Elizabethan Court and its Politics), G.R.Elton (Parliament) and Patrick Collinson (Elizabethan Church and the New Religion).

Simon Adams (ed.) *Queen Elizabeth I: Most Politick Princess* (1986)

A nice group of pithy essays by recent contributors to the historical debate on the Queen and her policies, including Peter Lake (Elizabethan Religious Settlement), Simon Adams (Foreign Policy) and J.P.Kenyon (Elizabeth and the Historians).

Christopher Haigh *Elizabeth I* (1988)

An excellent reassessment of Elizabeth I in the light of modern research, vigorously and entertainingly written, packed with shrewd and well-informed commentary on, and criticism of, the Queen and her achievements.